Pamper Your Partner

Pamper Your Partner

Thirty Days to a Romantic Relationship

Susan H. Hubbs

Writers Club Press

San Jose New York Lincoln Shanghai

Pamper Your Partner
Thirty Days to a Romantic Relationship

Writers Club Press
an imprint of iUniverse.com, Inc.

For information address:
iUniverse.com, Inc.
620 North 48th Street, Suite 201
Lincoln, NE 68504-3467
www.iuniverse.com

ISBN: 0-595-12984-6

Printed in the United States of America

To my husband, Rick, whose daily acts of love are a true inspiration to all that romance entails.

Contents

Preface

"We are all born with a box of matches inside.
We can't light them by ourselves.
The oxygen (to feed the flame) has to come from a lover's breath,
the candle (to provide the spark) can be anything:
a melody, a word, a caress, a sound.
Everyone has to discover what will pull his trigger to enable him to live,
because it is that explosive flare of the match that feeds our souls."

from "Like Water for Chocolate", a novel & motion picture
novel by Laura Esquivel, published 1990

Day #1

You've Got Mail!

Romantic Quote For Day #1

"True love is like ghosts, which everyone talks about and few have seen."

Francois, Duc de La Rochefoucauld
French writer and moralist (1613-1680)

Introduction

Are you in a relationship that has lost its excitement? Are you and your mate drowning in a quagmire of boredom? Can't seem to break out of the proverbial rut?

Get ready to change all of that, because you *can* bring the romantic spark back into your relationship! It is possible and has been proven that relationships will flourish and succeed, given the proper attention. Sadly, though, too many couples get past the courtship stage and forget the thrills, the pleasure, and the importance of romance.

"Pamper Your Partner" will demonstrate that it doesn't take a tremendous amount of effort to prevent you and your partner from becoming another disturbing relationship statistic. This book will perk up your relationship and reignite the fire between you and your partner!

Here's how it works:

You will be guided through one month of romantic gestures that require very little money and no extensive planning. Simply open up the book to Day #1 and follow the easy instructions! The romanticist inside you will begin to emerge as you read the romantic quote for the day. Then set all of your romance buttons into overload as you turn the page to discover today's romantic activity!

You can take all day to plan and accomplish your playful, loving gesture! Keep in mind that on occasional days, the book will suggest romantic ideas that require a purchase of some sort, however, there will always be an alternative penny-saving idea that doesn't cost a dime! Make use of the helpful "Notes" page which is provided for each activity.

Once you start the book, make every effort to continue on for the next twenty-nine days...try not to skip a day! If you find that your partner has to be out of town, or if an unexpected emergency arises, sneak a note into his suitcase, make phone calls, or arrange for flowers or candy to be delivered. The point is, don't let a single day go by without accomplishing a simple, loving gesture. When your mate arrives home and the household returns to normal, continue with the book where you left off.

Whatever happens, don't make the mistake of putting romance on the back burner. Make time for your partner, your relationship, and keep those loving feelings alive! Allow romance to become a ritual and you'll enjoy the benfits for years to come!

Romantic Activity For Day #1

Place "I Love You" notes everywhere! Be inventive and use your imagination. Leave a message perched on the dashboard of your mate's car that reads, "*You drive me wild!*"

Other suggestions:

On the television remote: "*You push all the right buttons!*"
On her bathroom mirror: "*You are so beautiful to me.*"
On the alarm clock: "*I love waking up next to you.*"
On the coffeepot: "*Good morning, my love.*"
On his soccer ball: "*I get a kick out of you!*"
On the light switch, "*You always turn me on!*"

Put "I Love You" notes in his briefcase, on the shower door/shower curtain, on her computer, on his cellular phone, inside her wallet, and anywhere else your lover is likely to see. Overload on romance and put it right where it belongs…back into your relationship!

NOTES

Phone calls to make:

Purchases:

Things To Do:

Day #2

Guess Who's Coming To Dinner?

Romantic Quote For Day #2

"Love doesn't grow on the trees like apples in Eden...it's something you have to make. And you must use your imagination to make it too..."

Joyce Cary
British novelist (1888-1957)

Romantic Activity For Day #2

Set up a small, intimate table in your bedroom, complete with tablecloth, candles, champagne and strawberries, or wine and cheese if that's what your partner prefers. Break out your finest dinnerware and spend some time conversing in this romantic atmosphere. Recall your first date, your first kiss, your first love-making session.

Warning! This assignment may lead to reenactments!

Other suggestions:

Substitute sparkling cider if no alcohol is desired.
Present a variety of fresh fruit in addition to the cheese.
Don't let the conversation drift to work, children, or anything other than the two of you!

Penny Saver For Day #2

Rather than splurging on pricey champagne and strawberries that may be out of season, simply set up your usual evening meal by candlelight. You're going to eat anyway, so the cost will be absorbed by your grocery budget!

NOTES

Phone calls to make:

Purchases:

Things To Do:

Day #3

Another Day
In Paradise

Romantic Quote For Day #3

"Whoso loves believes the impossible."

Elizabeth Barrett Browning
English poet (1806-1861)

Romantic Activity For Day #3

Today, you will pamper your partner in a way that no fancy, expensive day spa ever could! First, you'll need to clean up the bathroom. (Sorry, but nothing kills the mood more than mold and mildew!)

Next, make the atmosphere relaxing and sensual. While you are running the bathtub full of water, set out candles and piles of warm, fluffy towels. (You can have these preheating in the dryer!)

Now the fun begins! Indulge your mate in a bath he'll never forget. Take your time washing his hair, massaging her scalp and rinsing with warm water. This feels wonderful to both men and women! Use a soapy bath brush, loofah sponge or soft washcloth to lather up your partner from head to toe. If you feel comfortable, (and your partner isn't terrified!), get out the shaving cream and *carefully* give him a shave. Her legs aren't off limits either!

Finally, use those warm towels to dry your beloved's skin. Pat gently, don't rub too vigourously. Remember, this is supposed to be a sensual experience, not a workout!

Suggestions:

Use bubble bath if it would please your partner.

NOTES

Phone calls to make:

Purchases:

Things To Do:

Day #4

The Way We Were

Romantic Quote For Day #4

"I wept as I remembered how often you and I had tired the sun with talking and sent him down the sky".

William J. Cory
English poet (1823-1892)

Romantic Acitivity for Day #4

First, purchase a scrapbook for keeping momentos of your life together.

Next, spend some time with your partner searching your home for special memorabilia that you have saved from special dates and other events in your lives as a couple. Include ticket stubs, cards, theatre programs, old love letters, dried flowers, and any other keepsakes you treasured enough to preserve. Spread your momentos out on the floor or a table. Begin putting the scrapbook together while reminiscing about those private memories. Keep the scrapbook accessible and continually add to it!

Penny Saver for Day #4

If you can't purchase a scrapbook today, take the time to explain the plan to your mate. You can still spend the evening looking for those momentos and enjoying your memories. Look around the house for a box that will hold all your goodies. When you are able to purchase the scrapbook, everything will be organized and ready to assemble!

NOTES

Phone calls to make:

Purchases:

Things To Do:

Day #5

Addicted To Love

Romantic Quote For Day #5

"Pains of love be sweeter far
Than all other pleasures are."

John Dryden
English poet, dramatist (1631-1700)

Romantic Activity for Day #5

What do you do that drives your lover up the wall? You know. That nasty little habit you're always being reminded of? It may be something that threatens your health, like smoking or chewing tobacco. It may be that you're not as vigilant as you should be about wearing your seatbelt. Or it could be something as simple as leaving wet towels on the floor.

Whatever it is, beginning today, become more aware of that one annoying habit and make a vow to your mate that you will stop doing it…at least for the rest of this month. Chances are, if you can accomplish this feat for the next twenty-five days, you may have it beat!

What? You don't think this qualifies as a romantic activity? Just look at the gleam in your partner's eyes when you divulge what you will be giving up. Then you can tell me it's not a loving gesture!

NOTES

Phone calls to make:

Purchases:

Things To Do:

Day #6

Sunset Boulevard

Romantic Quote For Day #6

"I think true love is never blind,
But rather brings an added light,
An inner vision quick to find
The beauties hid from common sight."

Phoebe Cary
American poet (1824-1871)

Romantic Activity For Day #6

After dinner this evening, take a quiet stroll. Don't talk about bills or Johnny's bad report card. This is your special time. Tell your partner all the reasons why you are madly in love. Hold hands at every opportunity. Oh...and kissing is mandatory! Go ahead...maybe you'll give the nosy neighbor some ideas!

NOTES

Phone calls to make:

Purchases:

Things To Do:

Day #7

That's Entertainment!

Romantic Quote For Day #7

"Oh, you've got to remember the love.
You know love is a gift from up above.
Spread love, give love, share it now.
Measure your life in love."

"Seasons of Love" from the Musical RENT
Musical by Jonathan Larson

Romantic Activity For Day #7

Remember the early stages of your romance? Chances are, you went to the movies, and probably more than once. Tonight, you will relive those days by making a movie theatre, right in your own home. First, go out and rent a romantic video.

Some suggestions:
Casablanca
You've Got Mail
Romeo and Juliet
When Harry Met Sally
Ghost
Sleepless in Seattle
The Way We Were

Hand write an invitation to this evening's romantic event. Include a time, name of the movie, place to meet (i.e. den, family room, bedroom), and code of dress. Have the "cinema" set up with popcorn, drinks, blankets and pillows. Don't forget a box of tissues…just in case! Turn down the lights, snuggle with your honey, and…ACTION!!

Penny Saver For Day #7

No cash for a movie rental? Find a love story on television. If there isn't one on tonight, search the television guide for a night when a romantic movie will be shown. You have my permission to save this activity for that day! Meanwhile, for today's activity, move on to Day #8. It won't hurt to juggle around the activities, as long as you don't skip a day!

NOTES

Phone calls to make:

Purchases:

Things To Do:

Day #8

Terms of Endearment

Romantic Quote For Day #8

"Did my heart love 'til now?
Forswear it sight, for I never saw true beauty 'til this night."

William Shakespeare
English author (1564-1616)

Romantic Activity For Day #8

Compliments make the world go 'round.

Hmm…that doesn't sound exactly right. But for today's romantic gesture, it certainly fits! Start off the day by complimenting your partner's choice of clothing/hair. Keep it up throughout the day by pointing out the yummy breakfast, clean house, great campaign slogan, and/or the neatly mowed yard. You get the idea.

There's only one catch. You absolutely can't sound phony! The trick is to be subtle. Done to the extreme, this activity will seem less than genuine. So carefully pick when, where, and what you compliment. Remember, it's a wonderful feeling to know that your partner admires and appreciates you!

NOTES

Phone calls to make:

Purchases:

Things To Do:

Day #9

The Object
Of My Affection

Romantic Quote For Day #9

"The supreme happiness of life is the conviction that we are loved."

Victor Hugo
French novelist, poet, & dramatist (1802-1885)

Romantic Activity For Day #9

Purchase a romantic card, nothing silly or funny…not today. Take your time and choose the perfect card, one that will have your partner reaching for a hankie.

Inside the card, include a handwritten letter that describes your most romantic thoughts and feelings. Leave the card somewhere that your partner is sure to notice. Or you may want to read the letter to your beloved mate. Don't be shy and don't hold back!

Penny Saver For Day #9

Make your own card. On the outside, paste a picture of the two of you together.

NOTES

Phone calls to make:

Purchases:

Things To Do:

Day #10

Pandora's Box

Romantic Quote For Day #10

*"I hold it true, whate'er I befall; I feel it, when I sorrow most...
'Tis better to have loved and lost than never to have loved at all."*

Alfred Lord Tennyson (1809-1892)
"In Memoriam," 1850, stanza 4, line 27

Romantic Activity For Day #10

Today you are going to make your partner a "box of love." All during the day, jot down uplifting and optimistic phrases and ideas. Include the many reasons why you love your mate. Write down on paper why you think your partner is such a terrific person! You will need to put each idea on a separate piece of paper.

Next, search around the house or office for a cardboard box. (A shoe box would be perfect!) Decorate the box with romantic wrapping paper or simply cut out hearts and glue them onto the outside of the box. While wrapping and decorating, remember that the box is going to be opened up from time to time, so make it accessible!

Finally, fill the box with your "love notes" and present it to your lover, perhaps while you are relaxing after dinner. Explain that whenever a bad day rolls around, or if the blues hit unexpectedly, they should open the "love box", pick out one slip of paper and read it.

Hint: Make sure to keep the box full! An empty "love box" would make a bad day even worse!

NOTES

Phone calls to make:

Purchases:

Things To Do:

Day #11

Boogie Nights

Romantic Quote For Day #11

*"Three grand essentials to happiness in this life are
something to do, something to love, and something to hope for."*

Joseph Addison (1672-1719)
English essayist, poet, statesman

Romantic Activity For Day #11

Dance and romance!

Make some phone calls today and find a local dance club that provides a romantic atmosphere. A cozy jazz club would be great, or you could check out the coffee house on the corner that the two of you have been aching to try. Just make sure that the spot you choose has a dance floor and that the music is conducive to romance. You can plan on having a long, luxurious dinner, just order appetizers and drinks, or simply revel in the atmosphere. The purpose is to romance your partner, so steer clear of noisy, raucous night spots. Even if you both enjoy the boisterous night life, tonight, go for tranquil excitement.

Penny Saver For Day #11

This activity doesn't have to cost anything, but if you choose, you can stay home and dance to the tunes of a local radio station or delve into your private music collection. Use candles and a special tablecloth to set up your own version of that quiet little bistro. Just remember to keep the evening slow and seductive!

NOTES

Phone calls to make:

Purchases:

Things To Do:

Day #12

Can't Hardly Wait

Romantic Quote For Day #12

"Life is short and we have never too much time for gladdening the hearts of those who are traveling the dark journey with us. Oh be swift to love, make haste to be kind."

Henri-Frederic Amiel (1821-1881)
Swiss philosopher, poet

Romantic Activity For Day #12

Pick up the telephone several times during the day just to say "I Love You". Don't have a long conversation. Don't ask your mate to pick up milk or bread on the way home. Just say, "I love you". You can follow that up with a simple, "I can't wait to see you again." Then hang up. Do this a couple of times, but only if their job allows it. You can try a variation of this on beepers, mobile phones, voice mail, and e-mail.

Make that call…just because you love them!

NOTES

Phone calls to make:

Purchases:

Things To Do:

Day #13

Fantasia

Romantic Quote For Day #13

"Where there is love, there is life."

Mahatma Gandhi (1869-1942)
Indian spiritualist, political leader, humanitarian

Romantic Activity For Day #13

Sometime during the day, visit a travel agent's office and load yourself down with brochures and pamphlets that feature dream vacations. Gather information on a variety of destinations. (skiing, beaches, cruises, Europe, etc.)

Tell your partner that some day in the not too distant future, you want to share a special, romantic vacation with him/her. Explain that you want to start planning now, so that the two of you can enjoy this dream get-away!

Have fun going over all of the brochures. Ask your partner for input on any ideas that you might have overlooked. Narrow your choices down to two or three of your mutual favorites. You can always make the final decision at a later date.

Next, go over your budget and commit to putting away a certain amount from each paycheck toward your vacation. You may decide to set up an empty jar to deposit any loose change. Decorate the jar with brochure pictures of favorite vacation spots.

Above all, don't fuss and argue about your budget or the destination. Approach this from a fun standpoint and leave potential trouble spots up in the air. Just allow your partner to dream!

NOTES

Phone calls to make:

Purchases:

Things To Do:

Day #14

Close Encounters
Of The Best Kind

Romantic Quote For Day #14

"You know very well that love is, above all, the gift of oneself!"

Jean Anouilh
French playwright, screenwriter, director (1910-1987)

Romantic Activity For Day #14

Mmmm…Don't massages feel wonderful?

Today your mission of love involves learning a bit about the art of massage, and then practicing what you've learned. The best possible scenario requires a visit to your local video store where you can rent a video on the techniques of massage. Spend your lunch break soaking up the basics, then write up and deliver an "appointment card" to your mate. The appointment card should specify the time, place and dress code. (Instruct your partner to wear only a towel!)

Finally, get out the candles and practice your newly found skill!

Reminder:

If this is an activity you want to work on for several days, it's okay to move on to another activity for today if you want to!

Penny Saver For Day #14

No extra cash for a video? Stop by the library and check out a book on massage. Many of these books are highly instructiona. and have excellent pictures!

NOTES

Phone calls to make:

Purchases:

Things To Do:

Day #15

The Waterboy

Romantic Quote For Day #15

"Neither a lofty degree of intelligence
nor imagination nor both together
go to the making of genius.
Love, love, love, that is the soul of genius."

Samuel Adams (1722-1803)
American revolutionary

Romantic Activity For Day #15

Okay...it's been awhile since you've had any bathtime fun! Purchase a variety of special soaps, a bath brush or loofah sponge, and other bath goodies. You'll also need to pick up several stems of roses. Place the bath items inside a basket and set it just outside the shower.

Before your mate arrives home, use the dryer or a heating pad to warm a few towels. Strip the petals from the flowers and make a trail from the front door to the shower. When your partner arrives home, the trail will lead the way to you and the basket. Be ready to share in the fun!

Penny Saver For Day #15

Forget the basket! Make a path of paper hearts which leads to you and a steaming shower! Use whatever soap and bath supplies you already own to have a bit of good, clean fun!

NOTES

Phone calls to make:

Purchases:

Things To Do:

Day #16

Love Story

Romantic Quote For Day #16

"She gave me eyes, she gave me ears;
And humble cares, and delicate fears;
A heart, the fountain of sweet tears;
And love, and thought, and joy."

William Wordsworth
English poet (1770-1850)

Romantic Activity For Day #16

Today, grab your partner and take a drive to the local bookstore. Browse around together and choose a book you both would enjoy. When the two of you climb into bed tonight, one of you should begin to read the book aloud. Try to read a chapter every night, with the two of you taking turns.

Suggestion:

The "listener" can treat the reader to a foot massage during the reading!

Penny Saver For Day #16

Check out a library book!

NOTES

Phone calls to make:

Purchases:

Things To Do:

Day #17

Braveheart

Romantic Quote For Day #17

*"You say that love is nonsense…I tell you it is no such thing.
For weeks and months it is a steady physical pain, an ache about the
heart never leaving one, by night or by day; a long strain on one's
nerves like toothache or rheumatism, not intolerable at any one instant
but exhausting by its steady drain on the strength."*

Henry Brooks Adams (1838-1918)
American historian, writer

Romantic Activity For Day #17

Publicly profess your love!

Radio stations these days can be downright crazy and are usually up for anything. Call in and tell them that your goal is to treat your partner to one romantic gesture every day for thirty consecutive days. Surely this will intrigue someone! Ask if they will assist you by calling your mate at work (or home), and then allow you to declare your love, live on the air!

Or perhaps they will allow you to read a love poem over the air to your beloved. A good time to plan the event would be while you are both at home, so you can be assured that your partner is listening!

If one station turns you down, keep trying. Your reward will be worth it!

Suggestion:

Make a tape recording of the event!

NOTES

Phone calls to make:

Purchases:

Things To Do:

Day #18

Back To The Future

Romantic Quote For Day #18

"The pleasure of love is in loving."

Francois, Duc de La Rochefoucauld
French writer and moralist (1613-1680)

Romantic Activity For Day #18

Tonight's the night to go back in time…say about one hundred years!

Don't worry too much, though. No horse and buggy are required, but you will have to give up several modern day conveniences to set the proper mood.

This evening you and your partner will unplug the television, shut off all lights, disconnect the telephone, the beeper, and every other electrical distraction. Get out the candles, focus on each other, and enjoy the initimate atmosphere that you have created!

NOTES

Phone calls to make:

Purchases:

Things To Do:

Day #19

Breathless

Romantic Quote For Day #19

"How do I love thee? Let me count the ways.
I love thee to the depth and breadth and height
My soul can reach, when feeling out of sight
For the ends of Being and ideal Grace."

Elizabeth Barrett Browning
English poet (1806-1861)

Romantic Activity For Day #19

Learn to say "I Love You" in several languages. Use your newly found vocabulary with your partner throughout the day. On greeting cards or slips of paper, write down the foreign phrases you can't pronounce. Present them to your beloved at various times during the day and evening.

In addition, you can use sign language to express your love. With your right hand, hold your thumb out; your index finger and and pinkie fingers should point up. The two middle fingers should bend down into your palm. This is universal sign language which means "I Love You". Use it often!

Suggestions:

French: *Je t'adore*
German: *Ich liebe dich*
Greek: *S'ayapo*
Italian: *Ti amo*
Irish: *Taim i'ngra leat*
Spanish: *Te amo*

NOTES

Phone calls to make:

Purchases:

Things To Do:

Day #20

Tomorrow Never Dies

Romantic Quote For Day #20

"If music be the food of love, play on..."

William Shakespeare
English author (1564-1616)

Romantic Activity For Day #20

Make a list of all the things you'd like to do with your partner. These can be things to do today, tomorrow, next week, next year, and well into the future. The activities can be as simple as walking on the beach at dawn, or as elaborate as an Alaskan cruise! Keep in mind that these are activities that won't necessarily happen, but it's so much fun to dream!

Write or type your list, roll it up and tie with a ribbon. Present it to your partner, explaining that there are so many things you'd like for the two of you to experience, and this list contains but a few.

Being privy to your loved ones dreams is a very special blessing. Dare to let your partner in on yours!

NOTES

Phone calls to make:

Purchases:

Things To Do:

Day #21

Crimes Of The Heart

Romantic Quote For Day #21

"Praised be the fathomless universe,
For life and joy, and for objects and knowledge curious,
And for love, sweet love..."

Walt Whitman
American poet (1819-1892)

Romantic Activity For Day #21

Carve both sets of your initials into a tree in your yard.

Don't have a tree? Find some other wooden object…even a scrap of wood will work.

Tie a ribbon around the tree and attach a note that says, "*WOOD you be my everlasting love?*"

Or wrap the carved wood scrap in a box along with your love note.

Not the carving type? Use lipstick or a bar of soap to write your initials on the bathroom mirror. Draw a heart around the two sets of initials!

So easy to do, but unforgettable!

NOTES

Phone calls to make:

Purchases:

Things To Do:

Day #22

Pillow Talk

Romantic Quote For Day #22

"But true love is a durable fire,
In the mind ever burning,
Never sick, never old, never dead,
From itself never turning."

Sir Walter Raleigh
English writer (1554-1618)

Romantic Activity For Day #22

Buy a book of love poems. Browse through it and choose one that especially appeals to you then bookmark it. Wrap the book in a ribbon and leave it on your mate's pillow along with a few chocolate kisses.

After the ribbon is removed, mention that you'd like to read a poem aloud. Hold your partner's hand as you read. This will make your gift much more personal, not to mention memorable!!

Penny Saver For Day #22

Write your own poem and start your own "book" of poetry. In the future you can have it professionally bound as an eternal keepsake for your lover!

NOTES

Phone calls to make:

Purchases:

Things To Do:

Day #23

A Touch Of Class

Romantic Quote For Day #23

"In dreams and in love there are no impossibilities."

Janos Arany, (1817-1882)

Romantic Activity For Day #23

Do you both enjoy coin collecting? Gardening? Want to learn French before you take that dream vacation?

Make a list of clubs and courses that you think you'd both enjoy. Include the days, times, and cost (if any) of each activity. Be sure to include classes and activities that you would enjoy as a couple. If she hates bowling, don't put "Thursday Night Couple's Bowling League" on the list. If he is plagued with allergies, forget about the "English Rose Garden Club".

Tell your partner that you think it would be fun to join a club or take a class together. Pull out your list and ask your mate to select anything that sounds interesting. Listen to other suggestions that may be offered, then...sign up!

Penny Saver For Day #23

Although some classes require a nominal tuition, many are free! Also, numerous clubs are eager for your participation. Money is not always an issue!

NOTES

Phone calls to make:

Purchases:

Things To Do:

Day #24

A Night To Remember

Romantic Quote For Day #24

"If thou must love me, let it be for naught
Except for love's sake."

Elizabeth Barrett Browning
English poet (1806-1861)

Romantic Activity For Day #24

Pull out those old photographs and spend an evening living in the past!

First, purchase one or two new picture albums, then gather up all those loose snapshots that are collecting dust in drawers, shoeboxes, and envelopes. Grab a bottle of wine and spread out on a table or on the floor. Take your time reminiscing with your partner over the pictures. You'll have fun chuckling over those old clothes and hairstyles!

Next, begin to sort through the loose pictures and place them into new albums. Make a mental note of the pictures that your mate seems especially fond of. Pick one of these and next month, take it to be copied or enlarged. Purchase an appropriate frame and present the gift at a special time.

Penny Saver For Day #24

If cash is a problem, don't worry about buying new photo albums right now. Just spend the evening recalling fond memories as you review your old snapshots. You can still spend some time getting the loose photos in order. Make sure all pictures are labeled with names and dates!

NOTES

Phone calls to make:

Purchases:

Things To Do:

Day #25

The Paper Chase

Romantic Quote For Day #25

"I could not love thee, dear, so much,
Loved I not honor more."

Richard Lovelace
English poet (1618-c. 1657)

Romantic Activity For Day #25

Purchase brightly colored poster board and make several signs that will grab your mate's attention. "John loves Mary" and "I Love You, Mary" are a couple of suggestions. Decorate the posters with hearts, pretty ribbons, etc. Use your imagination!

Attach the posters to stakes and place them in the ground near the road where your partner is likely to see them while driving home from work or errands. You may want to get permission from neighbors to use their yards. Place the last sign in your yard and be ready for lots of hugs and kisses!

Suggestion:

Attach helium balloons to make the signs visible.

Penny Saver For Day #25

Instead of buying poster board, hit up your grocer for cardboard boxes. You can cut these apart and decorate them. If you decide to use the cardboard, you'll have to be extra creative to make them look nice…shabby, torn brown cardboard is NOT romantic!

NOTES

Phone calls to make:

Purchases:

Things To Do:

Day #26

Where Eagles Dare

Romantic Quote For Day #26

"Love rules the court, the camp, the grove,
And men below, and saints above,
For love is heaven, and heaven is love."

Sir Walter Scott
Scottish novelist (1771-1832)

Romantic Activity For Day #26

Grab your sweetie and go watch the planes take off and land. Yes…people actually do this!

Find a quiet spot near the airport where you can park the car. Then dream about the two of you taking off on a romantic excursion of your own. Cuddle up and talk about what you would do on this fantasy trip. Be outrageous with your ideas. Hold nothing back!

No bustling airport in your area? Take a drive to your local "inspiration point" or better yet, find one of your very own. You can still gaze at the stars and dream of that special getaway!

NOTES

Phone calls to make:

Purchases:

Things To Do:

Day #27

Heaven Can Wait

Romantic Quote For Day #27

"If love were what the rose is,
And I were like the leaf.
Our lives would grow together
In sad or singing weather."

Algernon Charles Swinburne
English lyrical poet (1837-1909)

Romantic Activity For Day #27

For this romantic gesture you'll need to purchase several flower bouquets and red construction paper. Cut out lots of red hearts. On some of these hearts write, "Cash in for one back rub", or "Good for one foot massage". Create coupons with your own ideas. Then write a sentimental note and attach it to one giant red heart.

Send your mate outside on some pretense, or better yet, prepare this while he/she is at work.

Place a few hearts and flowers at the entrance to your home. Scatter more hearts and flowers on the bed, in the bathroom, on the dining table. Set your giant heart in a place where it is sure to be seen. Advise your partner that some of the hearts are "special" love coupons!

Penny Saver For Day #27

Raid your flower garden, pick some wildflowers, or omit the flowers entirely. If construction paper is not in your budget, use whatever you can find around the house. Old greeting cards, typing paper, magazines…anything that can be shaped into a heart!

NOTES

Phone calls to make:

Purchases:

Things To Do:

Day #28

Star Trek

Romantic Quote For Day #28

"Give all to love;
Obey thy heart."

Ralph Waldo Emerson
American essayist and poet (1803-1882)

Romantic Activity For Day #28

Pitch a tent in the backyard. Get a friend to help, if necessary.

Fill the tent with sheets, blankets, and pillows. Set one blanket out on the grass and spend the evening on your backs, staring up at the stars, and holding hands. If the bugs become pesky you can always climb into the tent for some tender romance! Who knows? You may even decide to settle down and spend the night!

Suggestions:

Bring a well-stocked picnic basket filled with wine, cheese, and candles. (Don't forget the matches!)

Develop a new kissing technique and name it!

Penny Saver For Day #28

Don't have a tent? Borrow one from a camping friend, or simply forget the tent altogether. You can still set up blankets and pillows under the stars for a night of romance!

NOTES

Phone calls to make:

Purchases:

Things To Do:

Day #29

Treasure Island

Romantic Quote For Day #29

"Love seeketh not itself to please,
Nor for itself hath any care,
But for another gives its ease
And builds a Heaven in Hell's despair."

William Blake
English poet (1757-1827)

Romantic Activity For Day #29

Send your partner on a treasure hunt!

Cut up ten pieces of paper and on each one, write a message which directs your mate to a new location. Leave messages in the mailbox, tacked onto trees, on the lawnmower, etc. You can send your partner on a wild hunt around the neighborhood, around your yard, or anywhere outside of your home. The last note should instruct your mate to enter the house through a door of your choosing, where you will be waiting with open arms and a special gift!

Penny Saver For Day #29

Instead of buying a gift, let yourself be the present! Use your imagination! Welcome your partner back into the house dressed in ribbons and bows…or nothing at at all! Make up a special gift tag on which you have written instructions or a poem. Hang the tag from any body part!

Day #30

From Here To Eternity

Romantic Quote For Day #30

"True love's the gift which God has given
To man alone beneath the heaven;
It is not fantasy's hot fire,
Whose wishes, soon as granted, fly;
It liveth not in fierce desire,
With dead desire it doth not die;
It is the secret sympathy,
The silver link, the silver tie,
Which heart to heart and mind to mind
In body and in soul can bind."

Sir Walter Scott
Scottish novelist (1771-1832)

Romantic Activity For Day #30

Congratulations! After tonight, you will have completed thirty consecutive days of romancing your partner! This evening, you will take your partner out for a special dinner, but you'll need to prepare a few things ahead of time.

First you will need four sheets of paper and four envelopes. On each of three papers, write a different romantic thought, preferably something personal. On the fourth paper, use your most creative romantic feelings and write a short love letter. End the note with something which leads to a toast. (i.e. *"Let us begin this evening with a toast to romance, and to a future filled with love!"*)

Next, label each envelope 1, 2, 3 and 4, then insert the proper paper into its corresponding envelope.

Now for the plan:

After being seated at the restaurant, excuse yourself for a moment. Locate your server and ask him/her to deliver envelopes 1-4 to your dinner partner at the beginning of each course (i.e. envelope #1 should arrive with drinks, #2 with the appetizer, #3 with the main course, and #4 with dessert.) If you want to splurge, have a long-stemmed rose delivered with each note.

When the fourth and final envelope arrives, be prepared for a loving toast. Pre-order a bottle of wine, champagne, or sparkling cider!

Good luck and have fun!

Penny Saver For Day #30

If the expense of dinner in a restaurant is out of the question, stop by the store and pick up your partner's favorite meal. Enjoy this special dinner at home with you as the server! You can still prepare four notes and deliver them personally with each course!

NOTES

Phone calls to make:

Purchases:

Things To Do:

www.ingramcontent.com/pod-product-compliance
Lightning Source LLC
Chambersburg PA
CBHW020237290526
45784CB00003B/1003